ZEUS

B. A. Hoena

Consultant:
Dr. Laurel Bowman
Department of Greek and Roman Studies
University of Victoria, British Columbia

Capstone
press

Mankato, Minnesota

This ancient statue shows Zeus holding a thunderbolt in his right hand. As ruler of the heavens, Zeus used lighting as a weapon.

ZEUS

In Greek myths, Zeus (ZOOSS) was ruler of the heavens. He controlled the weather. He used thunder and lightning as weapons. In Roman myths, Zeus was known as Jupiter (JOO-puh-tur).

Zeus ruled the Olympians. Ancient Greeks and Romans believed these 12 powerful gods lived on Mount Olympus. This mountain is in central Greece. People believed the gods controlled every part of their lives.

Zeus had many duties as ruler of the Olympians. He created laws for gods and people. He made gods and people keep the promises they made. Zeus also protected travelers and beggars. He made sure these people were treated well.

In myths, Zeus is known as the father of gods and heroes. He is the father of several of the Olympians. Zeus also is the father of many important people in Greek myths.

GREEK and ROMAN *Mythical Figures*

Greek Name: **APOLLO**
Roman Name: **APOLLO**
Zeus' son and god of youth
and music

Greek Name: **ARES**
Roman Name: **MARS**
Zeus' son and god of war

Greek Name: **ARTEMIS**
Roman Name: **DIANA**
Zeus' daughter and goddess of
the hunt and the Moon

Greek Name: **ATHENA**
Roman Name: **MINERVA**
Zeus' daughter and goddess
of wisdom

Greek Name: **DIONYSUS**
Roman Name: **BACCHUS**
Zeus' son and god of wine

Greek Name: **HEPHAESTUS**
Roman Name: **VULCAN**
Zeus' son and god of fire

Greek Name: **HERA**
Roman Name: **JUNO**
Zeus' wife and goddess of
marriage and childbirth

Greek Name: **HERMES**
Roman Name: **MERCURY**
Zeus' son and messenger of
the gods

ABOUT MYTHOLOGY

The word myth comes from the Greek word *mythos*. This word means tale or story. But myths were more than just stories to ancient people. They used myths to explain the world around them.

The myth of the mountain nymph Echo is one example. Echo was always talking. One day as the goddess Hera (HER-uh) was searching for Zeus, Echo's constant talking angered Hera. Hera then made it so Echo could only repeat what others had just said to her. This myth explained why people heard echoes in the mountains. People thought the mountain nymph Echo was repeating their words.

Ancient Greeks and Romans believed the gods controlled nature. They often prayed to certain gods for help. They prayed to Demeter (de-MEE-tur), the goddess of growing things, for good harvests. They prayed to Zeus for rain. As god of the heavens, he controlled the weather.

In *Saturn Devouring his Children*, Simon Hurtrelle shows the ancient god eating one of his children. Saturn was the Roman name for Cronus.

THE BIRTH OF ZEUS

Before Zeus, the Titan Cronus (KROH-nuhss) ruled the heavens. He was married to the Titaness Rhea (REE-uh). Cronus also was Zeus' father.

Cronus' mother told him that one of his children would overthrow him. To prevent this, Cronus ate his children right after they were born. The children did not die. They were immortal. Cronus only trapped them in his stomach.

Cronus' actions angered Rhea. She wanted her children to be free. When Zeus was born, Rhea tricked Cronus. Rhea gave Cronus a rock covered in blankets to eat instead of Zeus. Rhea then hid Zeus on the island of Crete. There, nymphs raised him.

After Zeus grew up, he tricked Cronus into throwing up the children he had swallowed. Zeus and his siblings then escaped to Mount Olympus. There, they became known as the Olympians.

This ancient Greek sculpture was made around 500 B.C.
It shows the marriage of Zeus and Hera.

BATTLE OF THE GODS

The Olympians were glad to be free of Cronus. Yet they knew they were not safe. Cronus might swallow them again. The Olympians decided to fight Cronus and the other Titans for control of the world.

It seemed unlikely that the Olympians would win the battle. The Titans outnumbered them. But some of the Titans decided to help the Olympians. They did not like Cronus. Cronus' brothers the 100-handed giants and the Cyclopes (sye-KLOH–peez) also helped the Olympians.

After 10 years of fighting, the Olympians won the battle. Zeus and his brothers then decided who would rule each part of the world. Zeus chose the heavens. Poseidon (poh-SYE-duhn) ruled the seas. Hades (HAY-deez) was left with the Underworld.

Zeus gave his sisters duties as well. Demeter became the goddess of growing things. Hestia (HESS-tee-uh) became the goddess of the home. Zeus married Hera, and she became the goddess of marriage and childbirth.

Zeus punished
Prometheus by
chaining him
to a mountain.
Each day of his
punishment, a
vulture came to
eat his liver.
Since Prometheus
was immortal, his
liver grew back
each night.

ZEUS AND PROMETHEUS

Zeus wanted the world to be filled with living creatures. He gave the Titans Prometheus (proh-MEE-thee-uhss) and Epimetheus (e-puh-MEE-thee-uhss) the task of making creatures. These brothers had helped Zeus defeat Cronus.

The brothers made creatures from earth and water. Epimetheus then gave each animal special gifts. He gave some animals fur to keep warm. He gave others teeth and claws to catch food.

Epimetheus did not save any gifts for men. Prometheus worried that men could not take care of themselves without any special gifts. He decided to teach them how to build homes, to read and write, and to farm. These skills set them apart from other creatures.

Prometheus also gave men the gift of fire. But this action angered the Olympians. They thought the gift of fire made men too strong. Zeus decided to punished Prometheus and chained him to a mountain.

Dante Gabriel Rossetti's painting *Pandora*
shows the evils escaping from Pandora's box.

PANDORA'S BOX

Zeus often punished those who he felt did something wrong. He punished Prometheus for giving fire to men. He also wanted to punish men for accepting the gift.

At the time, no women lived in the world. Zeus told his son Hephaestus (he-FESS-tuhss) to create a woman, Pandora (pan-DOR-uh). The gods gave Pandora gifts like beauty and music. These gifts would make men trust and accept her. But the gods also gave Pandora curiosity.

The gods handed Pandora a beautiful box. The box contained things like hunger, sickness and old age. The gods did not tell Pandora what was in the box. They just told her not to open it. Zeus then sent Pandora into the world of men.

Eventually, Pandora's curiosity made her open the box. All the evils in the box escaped into the world. These evils weakened men. They made men hungry, sick, and die of old age. The evils in Pandora's box were men's punishment for accepting the gift of fire from Prometheus.

Several of Zeus' (top center) children became Olympians. This painting by Francois Verdier shows Athena (left), Hermes (bottom center), and Artemis (right). Dionysus sits at Zeus' feet.

THE FATHER OF GODS

Zeus was the father of many gods. Zeus and Hera's sons, Ares (AIR-eez) and Hephaestus, became Olympians. Ares was the god of war. Hephaestus was the god of fire.

Zeus was not a loyal husband. He often had children with other goddesses, Titanesses, or mortal women. Some of these children became Olympians. Apollo (uh-PAH-loh) was the god of youth and music. His sister Artemis (AR-ti-mis) was the goddess of the hunt. Hermes (HUR-meez) was the messenger of the gods. He also guided dead souls to the Underworld. Athena (uh-THEE-nuh) protected heroes as the goddess of wisdom. Dionysus (dye-oh-NYE-suss) was the god of wine.

Zeus fathered many lesser gods as well. Nine of his daughters were called Muses (MYOOZ-ess). These sisters are known for their music, which brought joy to everyone who heard it. Each Muse inspired people in a certain art such as math, dance, or poetry.

Benvenuto Cellini's statue shows Perseus holding Medusa's head.
Even after her death, Medusa's gaze could turn people to stone.

THE FATHER OF HEROES

Not all of Zeus' children became gods. The children he had with mortal women often became important people in myths. Zeus had a daughter named Helen with the queen of Sparta, Greece. Myths say Helen was the most beautiful woman in the world. The Greeks and the people of Troy fought over her during the Trojan War. Many heroes died during this 10-year battle.

Some of Zeus' sons became heroes. Perseus (PUR-see-uhss) was famous for killing Medusa (me-DOO-suh). This monster had snakes for hair, and her gaze turned people to stone.

Hercules (HUR-kyoo-leez) was Zeus' strongest and most famous son. He achieved many great deeds in his life. He killed the many-headed hydra. He captured Cerberus (SUR-buh-ruhss). This three-headed dog guarded the entrance to the Underworld. After Hercules' death, Zeus brought him to Mount Olympus and made Hercules a god.

Artists often say a Muse inspired them. Paul Cezanne's painting (left) shows a Muse kissing a poet's forehead to inspire him. Below is the planet Jupiter. It is named after the ruler of the Olympians.

MYTHOLOGY TODAY

Mythical names are common in the modern world. Jupiter is the Roman name for Zeus. It also is the name of the largest planet in the solar system. The planet Saturn has moons called Titan and Epimetheus. The continent Europe is named after Europa, one of Zeus' lovers.

Groups of stars also are named after mythical figures. The constellation Gemini was named for Zeus' twin sons Castor (CASS-tor) and Pollux (POL-uhks). These brothers loved each other so much that they did not want to be apart. Zeus placed them in the sky to be side by side forever.

Today, people do not believe in Greek and Roman myths. These myths are now told for people's enjoyment. Many books have been written about myths. TV shows and movies retell the stories of Hercules and other mythical heroes. Myths also help people learn about ancient cultures.

Adriatic Sea

•Rome

ITALY

N
W • E
S

GREECE

•Troy

Aegean Sea

ITHACA

Thebes

Ionian Sea

Athens

Sparta

DELOS

KEY

•   City

🏛   Oracle of Delphi

⛰   Mount Olympus

▨   Region of Attica

CRETE

Mediterranean Sea

SCALE
Miles
0   100   200

0   100   200
Kilometers

WORDS TO KNOW

culture (KUHL-chur)—a people's way of life, ideas, art, customs, and traditions

curiosity (kyur-ee-AHSS-i-tee)—wanting to know something; Pandora wanted to know what was in the box the gods gave her.

Cyclops (SYE-klahpss)—a giant with one eye in the middle of its forehead

immortal (i-MOR-tuhl)—able to live forever

mortal (MOR-tuhl)—not able to live forever

nymph (NIMF)—a female spirit or goddess found in a meadow, a forest, a mountain, or a stream

Olympian (oh-LIM-pee-uhn)—one of the 12 powerful gods who lived on Mount Olympus in Greece

Titan (TYE-ten)—one of the giants who ruled the world before the Olympians

Underworld (UHN-dur-wurld)—the place under the ground where the souls of the dead went

READ MORE

Green, Jen. *Myths of Ancient Greece.* Mythic World. Austin, Texas: Raintree Steck-Vaughn, 2001.

Richardson, Adele D. *Hercules.* World Mythology. Mankato, Minn.: Capstone Press, 2003.

USEFUL ADDRESSES

National Junior Classical League
Miami University
Oxford, OH 45056

Ontario Classical Association
2072 Madden Boulevard
Oakville, ON L6H 3L6
Canada

INTERNET SITES

Track down many sites about Zeus.
Visit the FACT HOUND at *http://www.facthound.com*

IT IS EASY! IT IS FUN!

1) Go to *http://www.facthound.com*
2) Type in: 0736816135
3) Click on "FETCH IT" and FACT HOUND
   will find several links hand-picked by our editors.

Relax and let our pal FACT HOUND do the research for you!

INDEX